The Hebrides

PICTS

Dunnotar

Iona

SCOTS

Dumbarton

NORTHUMBRIA

Lindisfarne

BRITONS

Jarrow

York

Derby

WELSH
KINGDOMS

MERCIA

EAST
ANGLIA

London

WESSEX

CORNWALL

D0767364

3

Viking dawn

The year 793 began with bad **omens** – of thunder, lightning and famine. And then, one calm summer's day, some strange ships appeared off England's east coast.

Those ships were the first Viking **raiders** to reach Britain's shores. A fierce northern people, they landed on the island of Lindisfarne.

They burnt its **monastery** and hauled all its treasure back to their ships. Word of the attack spread terror all over Europe.

The following year, the raiders returned, attacking another wealthy monastery at Jarrow on the River Tyne. Others sailed round the coast of northern Scotland and struck the Hebrides, including the great monastery at Iona.

Who were the Vikings?

The Vikings were a seafaring people from **Scandinavia**. They weren't called Vikings to begin with. This word wasn't used until much later. At the time, most people in England called them Danes, because the Vikings who attacked England were mostly from Denmark. Others called them Northmen.

Scandinavia is surrounded by water and has a long, rugged coastline. It's also quite mountainous which meant that its people relied on their ships to get about. The sea was their highway and their shipbuilding skills were excellent.

During the 8th century, the **population** in Scandinavia was rising. Farming land was poor, so many men of fighting age went abroad to find new land to settle in. Britain attracted them because it was **fertile** as well as wealthy.

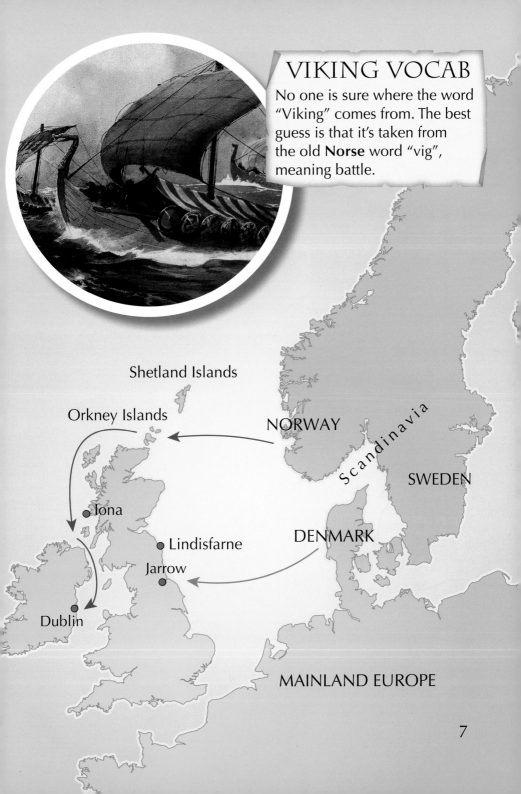

Shetland Islands

Orkney Islands

NORWAY

Scandinavia

SWEDEN

Iona

Lindisfarne

DENMARK

Jarrow

Dublin

MAINLAND EUROPE

The Viking longship

The Viking longship was the fastest, most powerful ship of its time.

It was built using overlapping wooden planks, which made it very strong. It was fitted with a mast, a large square sail, and oars along each side.

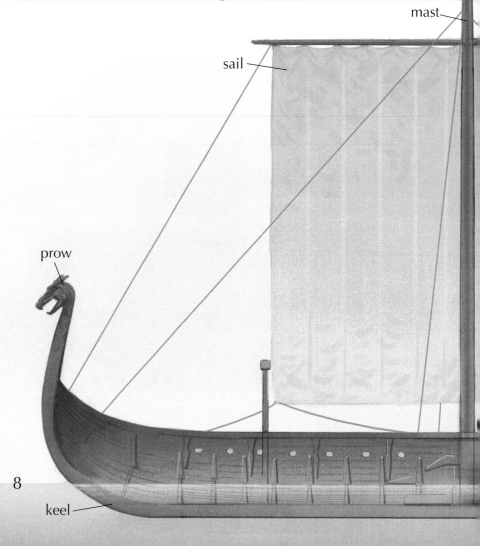

mast

sail

prow

keel

8

The longship was also double-ended, meaning that the prow and the stern were the same. This allowed the raiders to reverse out of trouble just as fast as they got into it. Its shallow keel meant that it could be sailed up rivers or hauled on to a beach. It was light too, so it could even be turned upside down and dragged over land.

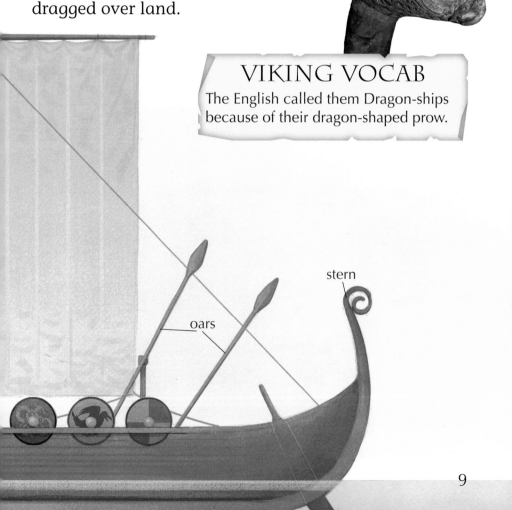

VIKING VOCAB

The English called them Dragon-ships because of their dragon-shaped prow.

stern

oars

Silver and slaves!

The Vikings weren't always raiding. They traded too.
When trading they used silver as money.
They sometimes chopped it up into bits, called
hack-silver. They also melted it down to make
arm rings. The number of arm rings a warrior wore
was a sign of his wealth and power.

The Silverdale Viking Hoard was found in Lancaster
in 2011 by a man with a metal detector. It contained
silver coins, arm rings, finger rings and brooches.

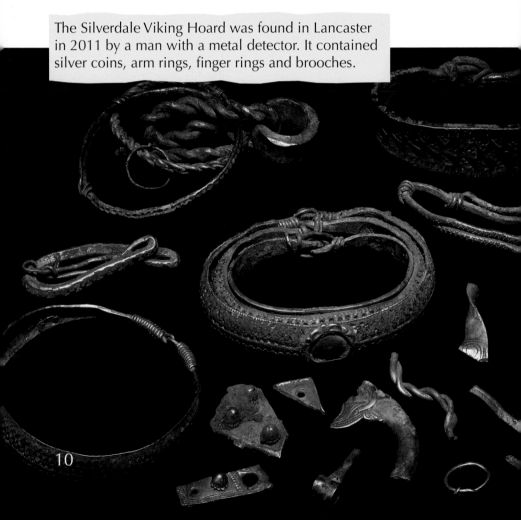

The Cuerdale Viking Hoard was found in Lancashire in 1840. It contained over 8,600 items including silver coins, arm rings, finger rings and brooches.

a viking slave collar

The Vikings took many captives during their raids. These were ordinary men, women and children, who were clapped in chains and then taken to big slave markets in Europe to be sold into slavery.

The Viking raids reached Ireland by 798. The raiders began to build **fortified** ports called longphorts, where they could spend the winter in safety. Many of these ports grew into great trading centres, like Dublin.

Invasion!

By 850, the Vikings were building bases on the coast of mainland Britain, in Kent and on the Thames. Their raids got bigger. Bands of Vikings began grouping together and more Vikings crossed the sea to join them.

Now the Vikings were strong enough to launch a full invasion. In the summer of 865, a fleet made up of hundreds of longships appeared off the British coast. They carried a great army made up of thousands of well-trained Viking warriors, led by a fierce chieftain called Ivarr the Boneless. Their aim was **conquest**.

Over the next few years, this army swept through England, destroying its Anglo-Saxon kingdoms one by one, until finally only Wessex remained.

These invaders also swept north. Viking armies stormed the capital of the Britons, Dumbarton, in 870, and the Pictish **stronghold** at Dunottar.

King Edmund of East Anglia was captured and killed by the Vikings during their conquest. He was soon made into a Christian saint.

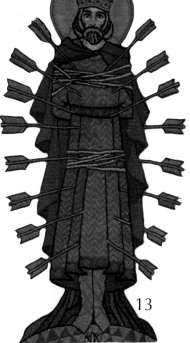

Into battle!

In battle, both the Vikings and the Anglo-Saxons formed their men into shield walls. This was a wall of shields, made up of three or more ranks of warriors standing shoulder to shoulder, holding their shields so that they overlapped each other.

VIKING VOCAB

Many Viking chiefs carried a war banner into battle. This was called a "raven banner". The raven was an important symbol for Vikings, as it was the symbol of the Viking god, Odin.

The two walls clashed against each other, and the battle was often decided by one shield wall breaking the other.

Most Viking warriors carried axes, spears and bows, along with a large, round wooden shield. Most were lightly armoured, wearing padded leather. Only important Vikings carried swords and wore proper armour like chain mail.

Viking settlers

The Viking leaders shared out much of the land they captured amongst their men, many of whom began farming.

Vikings were excellent farmers, sowing barley, rye and oats, and keeping animals.

Jarlshof in Shetland has one of the best preserved Viking **homesteads** in the British Isles. The Shetland Islands were amongst the first places in Britain to be settled.

Many of the native people fled or were forced out, but some stayed and lived under Viking rule. Some Vikings brought their wives and families with them to the new land. Others married local women and started new families. The settlers took over settlements that were already there, but they also started their own settlements.

A settler's home

A Viking's home was called a longhouse. This was a long, rectangular building with one big room. The roof was thatched and the walls were made of a mix of timber and **turf**.

At its centre was the hearth, which was used for cooking and heating. A metal pot would have hung over it, as well as a roasting spit. A hole in the roof let out smoke.

18

roasting spit

animal byre

bench

hearth

People slept on benches set against the inside wall.
One end was used as an animal **byre**. The animals
helped keep the house warm during the long
winter nights.

For entertainment, the Vikings told stories to each
other round the fire. Children played Hnefatafl, which
was a board game a bit like chess.

Life in Viking York

The Vikings captured York in 866, and it soon became their capital, known as Jorvik. It was a busy port and a **commercial** centre.

Jorvik's main street was called Coppergate, meaning "street of the cup-makers". It was a noisy, bustling place made up of closely-packed houses, stores and workshops. It was dirty and smelly too. Its narrow streets were polluted with human and animal waste.

tanner

cloth dyer

The **tanner** and the cloth dyer would have added to the stench. And the blacksmith's forge would have added heat and smoke. The antler-worker made domestic objects such as combs and knives out of deer antlers, while wood-turners made the cups and bowls that gave the street its name.

blacksmith

wood-turner

antler-worker

Viking gods

The Vikings who settled in the British Isles from the 8th century were pagans, which meant they didn't believe in the Christian God. They had their own gods. The most important Viking god was Odin, but the most popular Viking god was Odin's son, Thor, who was the god of thunder.

Odin, chief of the norse gods

Thor wielded a great hammer called Mjollnir. Many Viking warriors wore a small hammer round their necks, in the same way that Christian warriors wore a cross.

A Viking's **reputation**, and that of his **ancestors**, was very important. Viking legends, called sagas, kept alive the deeds of their gods, their heroes and their **forefathers**.

Viking burials

Vikings believed that when they died they would join the gods in the afterlife, so they were laid to rest with all the things they thought they would need. Men would have taken their weapons or tools. Women might have taken their jewellery. Food and drink was often included.

An important Viking might have been given a boat burial, like the one discovered on the coast at Ardnamurchan in Scotland.

The dead man was buried inside the hull of a timber boat, which was almost five metres long and one and a half kilometres wide. His wooden shield was laid over his chest. His sword and spear were at his side. He was surrounded by his most prized possessions, including a knife, axe, drinking horn, ring pin and a **whetstone**.

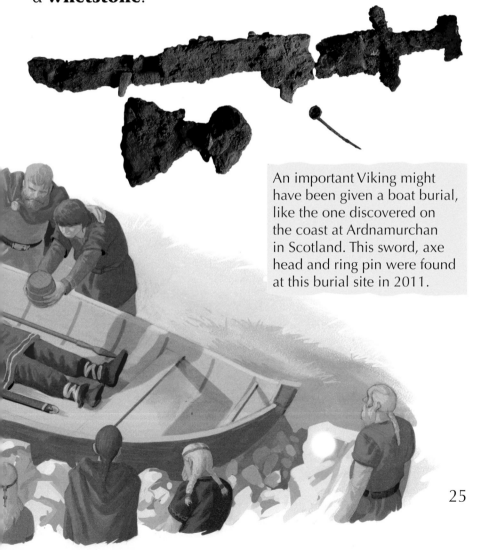

An important Viking might have been given a boat burial, like the one discovered on the coast at Ardnamurchan in Scotland. This sword, axe head and ring pin were found at this burial site in 2011.

Wessex alone

With the rest of England conquered, the Viking army turned towards Wessex.

Their first invasion in 871 ended in defeat after Wessex's army outfought them at the battle of Ashdown. Many thousands of Vikings were killed, including some of their leaders.

Wessex had a new king, whose name was Alfred.
His new reign faced many difficulties. In 878
the Vikings nearly captured him at Chippenham,
forcing him to flee into Athelney marshes. All seemed
lost, but Alfred refused to be beaten. He gathered his
army for one final battle for England's future.

That battle, at Edington, was a great victory for Wessex.
It marked the turn of the tide against the Vikings.

The Danelaw

In 880, soon after his victory at Edington, King Alfred signed a **treaty** with the Vikings which split England in two. The divide ran roughly along the line of an old Roman road called "Watling Street".

King Alfred discusses his treaty with Viking leaders.

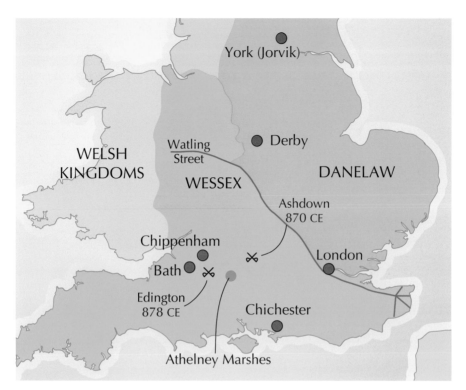

Mercia was cut in half – the southern part was for the Anglo-Saxons and the northern part was for the Vikings. East Anglia also went to the Vikings, but Alfred gained London.

The part ruled by the Vikings, which made up about a third of England, became known as the Danelaw.

The treaty meant that Wessex's borders were safe for now. But it also meant that in the Danelaw, Viking rule would last for generations.

Alfred the Great

The Vikings launched new attacks in 885 and 892, but these were beaten back easily. Wessex was getting stronger, mainly down to Alfred's skills as an **administrator**.

Alfred fortified a network of towns. Places like Bath and Chichester became strongholds, or **burhs**. No one would be more than 30 kilometres from one of these forts.

Alfred reorganised the army and set up a navy to defend the coast. He paid for this with new **taxes** and put in place a chain of loyal officials to help him. He rewarded good service fairly, with grants of land and titles such as knighthoods.

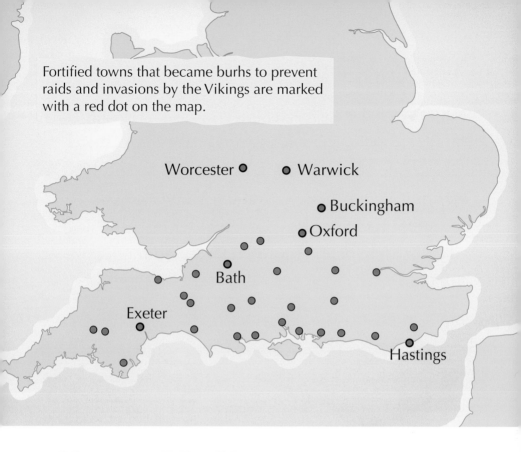

Fortified towns that became burhs to prevent raids and invasions by the Vikings are marked with a red dot on the map.

Worcester ●   ● Warwick

● Buckingham

● Oxford

Bath

Exeter

Hastings

Alfred improved the English coins and made the economy stronger.

The turn of the tide

King Alfred died in 899, but his children carried on his struggle. His son Edward pushed the area of Viking rule back bit by bit. Every town he captured was quickly fortified, so that the Vikings couldn't recapture them again. Alfred's daughter, Athelfled, ruled in Mercia. She captured Derby and other midland towns.

Edward's own son, Athelstan, pushed the Vikings back even further. He reconquered most of the land the Vikings had taken, including their capital, York.

In the north, the Viking threat pushed the warring Scots and Picts together. The first king of a united Scotland was Kenneth McAlpine in 843. He pulled together what troops the two sides had left and drove the invaders away.

Danegeld

During the late 10th century, the Viking attacks began again. England's ruler was King Athelred the Unready. In the summer of 991, the Vikings defeated Athelred's army at Maldon in Essex.

Athelred paid them 10,000 pounds of silver to stop their attacks and go home. A few years later, another Viking army **besieged** London. They were also paid off, this time with 16,000 pounds of silver.

Money used to pay off the Vikings became known as Danegeld. Unfortunately, it didn't work. It only encouraged the raiders to return, and each time they did, the price of peace went up. By 1012, it cost Athelred 48,000 pounds of silver. That's about the same weight as a fully laden double-decker bus.

The St Brice's Day Massacre

In his frustration, Athelred planned the **massacre** of all Viking settlers in England, who the English called "Danes". It took place on St Brice's Day on 13 November 1002. The slaughter was bloody. Many thousands of settlers were killed, including women and children, and many of their leaders.

It was a bold and reckless move, and it failed. The massacre enraged King Svein of Denmark, whose own sister was among the dead. He invaded with a large army. English resistance crumbled, and Athelred fled to France.

A burial pit was uncovered in Oxford in 2008 which held the remains of about 40 charred skeletons. They are thought to have been victims of the St Brice's Day Massacre.

Knut the Great

In 1017, Svein's son, Knut, became King of England. There was no one left in the Anglo-Saxon royal family to challenge him. He was the first Viking to rule the entire country.

While he was a strong king, he also ruled with a light touch. The people and the nobility were largely left alone. He was overseas a lot as England was just one part of his vast North Sea Empire.

He was also wise. One legend tells of how he became fed up with the flattery of his **courtiers**. He set his throne beside the seashore and let the waves slowly rise over his feet. He showed his men that even he was not powerful enough to command the tides.

Knut the Great was the most successful Viking of them all, ruling England in peace for 20 years.

The end of the Viking age

The last big Norse invasion was led by Norwegian Harald Hardrada in 1066. He landed in Yorkshire with a large Viking army. They met the forces of the English king, Harald Godwinson, at Stamford Bridge.

After a huge and bloody battle, the Vikings were wiped out.

Soon after, William the Conqueror landed in the south at the head of a **Norman** army to make his own claim to the throne. The exhausted English rushed south to meet him, but were defeated at the Battle of Hastings. Godwinson was killed and William took the throne.

1066 brought an end to the Viking age and the Anglo-Saxon age, and it also brought the beginning of the Norman age.

The Viking threat went on for a while longer in Scotland. Norse kings kept control over the north and west. In 1263 the Scots defeated King Hakon IV of Norway at Largs, which spelt the end of Scandinavian power there.

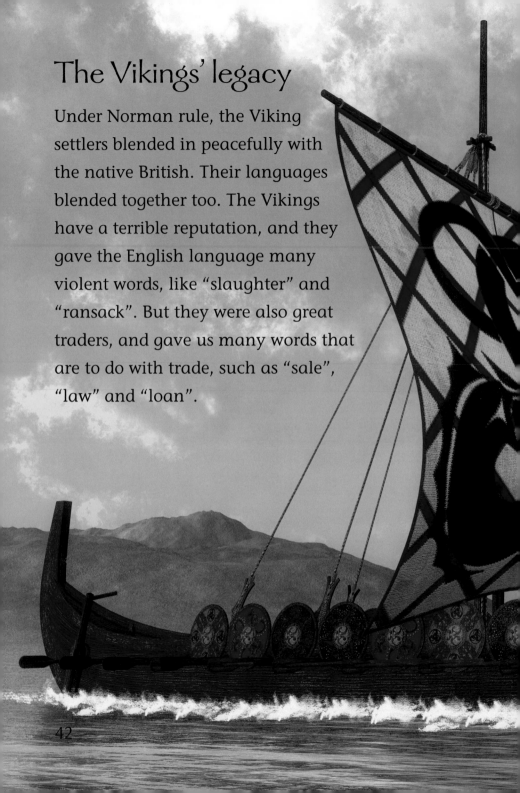

The Vikings' legacy

Under Norman rule, the Viking
settlers blended in peacefully with
the native British. Their languages
blended together too. The Vikings
have a terrible reputation, and they
gave the English language many
violent words, like "slaughter" and
"ransack". But they were also great
traders, and gave us many words that
are to do with trade, such as "sale",
"law" and "loan".

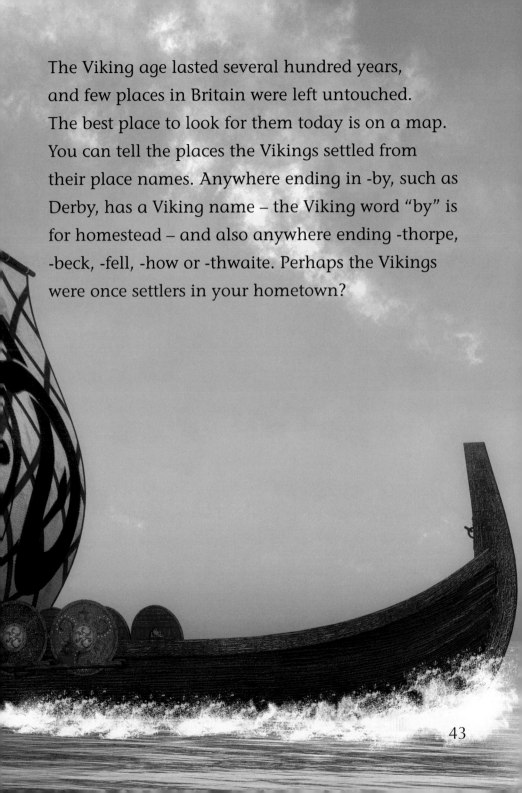

The Viking age lasted several hundred years, and few places in Britain were left untouched. The best place to look for them today is on a map. You can tell the places the Vikings settled from their place names. Anywhere ending in -by, such as Derby, has a Viking name – the Viking word "by" is for homestead – and also anywhere ending -thorpe, -beck, -fell, -how or -thwaite. Perhaps the Vikings were once settlers in your hometown?

Glossary

administrator someone who runs and organises things

ancestors and forefathers people who have come before you, such as your great-grandfather

besieged surrounded with a hostile army

burhs fortified settlements

byre a shelter for cows and other animals

commercial to do with business and trade

conquest defeat by force

courtiers attendants of a king or queen

fertile good for growing crops

fortified turned into a fort

homesteads houses, along with the land and other buildings that go with them, such as barns

massacre the killing of large numbers of people at once

migrated moved from one place to another

monastery a place where monks live

Norman a people descended from Vikings who colonised Normandy in the north of France; Norman comes from "Norseman"

Norse to do with Scandinavia

omens signs of what is coming in the future

population the number of people living in a place

raiders attackers who strike by surprise, steal and destroy, and then leave quickly

reputation what people think of you

Scandinavia Denmark, Norway and Sweden

stronghold a place that can be defended, like a fort

tanner a person who turns animal skins into leather, making goods such as shoes

taxes payments that must be made to the government

treaty an agreement between two sides

turf the top part of the soil, including the grass and roots

whetstone a type of stone used to sharpen swords

Index

Vikings in Britain timeline

793CE – The first Viking raid on the Northumbrian monastery at Lindisfarne takes place.

841CE – Viking longphorts established at Dublin, and other places in Ireland.

865CE – The 'Great Heathen Army' led by Ivar the Boneless lands in England.

866CE – Vikings capture York and make it their capital.

871CE – The Viking army attacks Wessex. Alfred becomes King.

878CE – Alfred defeats the Vikings at Edington.

880CE – Alfred signs a treaty with the Vikings, dividing England in half. The Danelaw is born.

920CE – King Edward of Wessex recaptures the Danelaw south of the Humber estuary.

927CE – King Athelstan captures York.

991CE – Wessex is defeated at the battle of Maldon, and Viking raids on England get worse. King Athelred the Unready begins paying large tributes, known as 'Danegeld'.

1002CE – The St Brice's Day Massacre takes place, when many Viking settlers are killed.

1017CE – Knut becomes King of England.

1066CE – The defeat of Harald Hadrada and the last great Viking army at Stamford Bridge. William the Conqueror leads the Norman Conquest at the Battle of Hastings.

1263CE – The battle of Largs, fought between the Scots and the Vikings under King Hakon IV, leads to the end of Viking dominance in the northern and western isles.

Ideas for reading

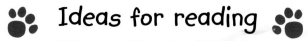

Written by Clare Dowdall, PhD
Lecturer and Primary Literacy Consultant

Reading objectives:
- retrieve and record information from non-fiction
- read books that are structured in different ways
- discuss their understanding and explain the meaning of words in context
- ask questions to improve understanding

Spoken language objectives:
- participate in discussions, presentations, performances, role play, improvisations and debates

Curriculum links: History – Viking raids and invasion

Resources: map, whiteboard, art materials for shield making, ICT for research, paper and pens

Build a context for reading
- Ask children what they know about the Vikings. Collect ideas as a thought shower on a whiteboard around the word *Vikings*.
- Look at the front cover and read the blurb together. Add new information to the thought shower.
- Look at the thought shower together. Based on existing knowledge, help children to raise questions to guide reading.
- Note their questions on another whiteboard for reference

Understand and apply reading strategies
- Turn to the contents. Discuss how the book is organised. Notice the chronological order and the key information about events, battles and individuals.
- Read pp2–3 aloud. Look at the map and challenge children to identify where they live now and what it was called in Viking times.